GEN Z
Goes to Work

Understanding & Engaging
Generation Z in the Workplace—
A Practical Guide and Workbook

DR. CHARLES V. BIERBRIER

Gen Z Goes to Work
Understanding & Engaging Generation Z in the Workplace—
A Practical Guide and Workbook

Copyright © 2024 by Dr. Charles V. Bierbrier

All rights reserved. No part of this book may be reproduced or transmitted in any form or by any means without written permission of the author.

ISBN: 978-1-0689417-0-2

Contents

Introduction 1
1 Workplace Generations 5
2 Challenges & Opportunities of Gen Z in the Workplace . . 17
3 Gen Z Work Value Preferences 27
4 Engaging Gen Z in the Workplace 39
5 Embracing the Future of Work with Gen Z 65

Complimentary Online Resources 77
Connect with the Author 79
About the Research 81
About the Author 83
Four Pillars for Gen Z Engagement 85
Complete Set of Worksheets 89
Bibliography 115

Introduction

As a researcher, business consultant, and professor, I have always been fascinated by the notion of generational differences. I experience this phenomenon firsthand when interacting with students in the classroom and dealing with employers in my consulting practice. These generational differences are not just anecdotal but supported by empirical evidence. These experiences have reinforced the importance of understanding and leveraging each generation's unique qualities for organizational success.

Today's workplace is undergoing a major transformation with the emergence of Generation Z (Gen Z), resulting in a significant generational shift. Gen Z will soon represent the majority of the incoming workforce and is expected to triple in size over the next decade. By 2030, it is forecasted to represent 30% of the U.S. workforce. Adapting to this new reality will be of vital importance for organizations to thrive in an ever-changing and competitive landscape.

Importance of Understanding Gen Z

Gen Z is the most culturally diverse, tech-savvy generation yet, and ignoring or misunderstanding this demographic shift may lead to missed opportunities for attracting and retaining top talent. Leveraging Gen Z within organizations will be essential to drive innovation and bring new perspectives to the workplace. Given today's dynamic work environment, employers must be able to successfully navigate these challenges while managing the complexities of an increasingly diverse workplace. By better understanding Gen Z, employers can bridge generational gaps in the workplace and facilitate collaboration and productivity in today's multigenerational work environment.

Managerial Implications

What does this mean for employers, managers, and human resources (HR) professionals? Well, first off, the recruitment and management strategies of the last 20 years may no longer be effective. In reality, what motivates one generational cohort may demotivate another, having a significant impact on rewards systems and other workplace motivators. Employers will need to examine their practices to create a more inclusive, dynamic, and productive multigenerational workforce. If not, they risk losing talent and reducing their competitive edge.

About This Book

The purpose of this book is to provide employers with insights and best practices for managing and understanding Gen Z. It is the result of extensive empirical research that I conducted as part of my doctoral study ("Work Values Preferences of Generation Z in the United States"). Using a quantitative research methodology, I examined the work values, or factors, that Gen Z considered most important in the workplace. Essentially, I identified what they place the highest importance on. My goal with this book is to summarize and present my findings straightforwardly, providing you with practical and actionable takeaways that you can use in today's workplace.

Who Should Read This Book?

This book is for anyone who is interested in better understanding Gen Z in the workplace, improving workplace dynamics, and leveraging Gen Z talent in a multigenerational workplace:

- **Employers & Managers**: You will gain insights to better recruit, retain, and motivate Gen Z talent within your organization.
- **HR Practitioners**: You will obtain valuable perspectives on Gen Z's values, enabling more effective strategies that are best aligned with their workplace expectations.
- **Business Leaders & Entrepreneurs**: You will understand the implications of today's multigenerational workplace and how to best leverage Gen Z's strengths and skills for organizational success.

- **Educators and Career Advisors**: You will learn and understand Gen Z's workplace expectations, in order to better prepare them for success as they embark on their careers.

Anyone interested in better understanding Gen Z and wishing to create a more collaborative and inclusive workplace culture will benefit from this book. My intent is to provide a practical guide full of useful evidence-based practices and involve you in the process.

How to Use This Book

At the end of each chapter, you will find reflective exercises designed for you to complete. This personal workbook and guide will help you better understand not only Gen Z but also yourself as you navigate a multigenerational work environment. Use these worksheets to reflect and apply the lessons discussed in each chapter. For convenience, I've compiled all the chapter worksheets at the end of this book for quick reference. Additionally, an online version of these worksheets (downloadable PDF) is available on my website at no charge. Simply visit https://www.bierbrier.com/resources for instant access.

One final thought before you begin your journey: I highly recommend reading the chapters in sequence and taking the time to perform the self-reflection exercises that follow. These exercises will significantly aid in developing your leadership and management techniques when interacting with Gen Z in today's multigenerational workplace.

CHAPTER ONE

Workplace Generations

The modern workplace is a melting pot of generational diversity, with each cohort bringing its own unique set of values, experiences, and expectations. Understanding these differences is crucial for fostering a harmonious and productive work environment. The study of generational differences is not new, having been discussed throughout history. Even as far back as Ancient Greece, Plato spoke of the difficulties understanding the behaviors of the younger generation. Today is no exception.

Generational Cohorts

A generational cohort is a group of individuals born within the same time period, typically 15–17 years, who share common historical, social, and cultural events during their formative years. These distinct cohorts have unique collective worldviews and values.

Understanding the generational cohorts and their characteristics has significant implications in the workplace. Different generations may have varying expectations for work–life balance, career advancement, and communication styles. By recognizing these differences, employers can develop more effective workplace strategies that enhance intergenerational communication. This understanding is crucial for shaping recruitment and retention strategies and developing workplace policies and practices that are inclusive of all generational cohorts.

The Different Cohorts in the Workplace

Several generational cohorts are active in the workplace, each with its own unique set of characteristics, values, and work styles. Let's briefly examine each cohort, highlighting important historical and social events to put each group into context.

Traditionalists/Silent Generation (born 1925–1945): This cohort was impacted by a range of world events, including the Great Depression, World War II, and the Korean War. As a result, they tend to be frugal, hardworking, and loyal to their employers. They value job stability and have a strong work ethic. Traditionalists prefer top-down management styles and conservative business environments. However, they may be less comfortable with technology and change and prefer more traditional forms of communication and work processes. As an aging population, they represent less than 1% of the workforce, with most having retired.

Those who continue to work often do so to stay socially connected and share their knowledge and expertise.

Baby Boomers (born 1946–1964): They were given this name as a result of the high birthrate after World War II and represent a significant presence in the workplace. Baby Boomers were impacted by the civil rights movement, Vietnam War, and Watergate scandal. They also witnessed the assassinations of Martin Luther King, Jr. and John F. Kennedy. Given that they lived through a time of economic growth and prosperity, Baby Boomers experienced job security and full employment. As one of the wealthiest cohorts, they are known to be optimistic, career driven, and likely to view their work as an extension of their identity and self-worth. They respect authority in the workplace and are patient for rewards and promotions. They are sometimes characterized as workaholics. Baby Boomers represent roughly 20% of the U.S. workforce, but their numbers are decreasing as many enter retirement.

Generation X (born 1965–1979): Gen X grew up in the shadow of the Baby Boomers and are also known as the "MTV" or "Latchkey" Generation. As the first generation to have a high proportion of two working parents, they are characterized as coming home after school to an empty house and having MTV babysit them, as they took care of themselves or their siblings. Gen X is the only generation that bridges the analog and digital world. They grew up with the introduction of the personal computer, so they are comfortable adopting new technologies. Gen X witnessed the collapse of the former

Soviet Union, endured times of economic uncertainty, and experienced higher rates of parental divorce than prior generations. This made them more pragmatic and direct. Unlike the Baby Boomers before them, Gen X prefer to "work to live" rather than "live to work." They are known for their independence, resilience, and adaptability. They represent roughly 31% of the U.S. workforce and are in their prime earning years.

Generation Y/Millennials (born 1980-1994): They are the first generation to have grown up alongside the evolution of the internet and social media. Having come of age during the digital era, they are highly tech savvy and interconnected. Gen Y grew up with mobile phones and email and have an ease with digital technology. Gen Y lived through the terror attacks on 9/11, witnessed the burst of the dot-com stock market bubble, and saw corporate ethics scandals unfold. This included the fall of major companies, such as Enron and Arthur Andersen. Unlike Gen X, Gen Y had much more supervision from parents, teachers, and coaches. This may explain why they have demonstrated higher levels of narcissism and often require more praise in the work environment. Gen Y live for the present and prefer experiences and travel over material possessions. They seek purposeful and meaningful work over salary and benefits and prefer casual dress and collaborative work environments. Gen Y are the largest cohort in the U.S. workforce, representing approximately 35%. They are assuming supervisory and management roles and stepping into leadership roles within organizations.

Generation Z (born 1995-2012): Gen Z, also known as "digital natives" or "iGen," is the first fully digital generation, as they have never known a world without social media or the internet. This makes them extremely tech savvy. Their formative years were marked by social justice movements, major technological advancements, and, most recently, a global pandemic, all of which has significantly impacted them. Many Gen Z members began their careers remotely, working from home via Zoom, unlike previous generations that began with in-person jobs.

Gen Z are also very concerned with global issues, such as social justice and climate change. In a recent Deloitte report, 59% of Gen Z said they worried about climate change. Gen Z also place a great importance on diversity, in terms of not only race and gender but also sexual orientation, making them more likely to adopt and accept gender-neutral pronouns. U.S. Gen Z are more ethnically diverse than any prior cohort, making them the last majority White/Caucasian generation.

Gen Z spend more time on electronic devices than previous generations, averaging over seven hours a day, which may hinder their in-person social skills. The Society for Human Resource Management reports that major employers, such as PwC, Deloitte, and KPMG, offer special training to help Gen Z improve communication skills, as they often lack "soft skills" and nonverbal communication abilities. The rise in social media use has also introduced new concerns for Gen Z, such as the fear of missing out (feeling excluded by what they view on social media). Gen Z have reported higher rates of anxiety, depression, and suicide compared to previous generations at the same age. Despite their global connectivity, Gen Z also report higher levels of loneliness.

Gen Z are more pragmatic and realistic about the world, making them more flexible and practical. They represent approximately 13% of the U.S. workforce and are the newest cohort.

Workplace Generations 2024

Generational Cohort Name	Birth Years	Key Characteristics
Traditionalists/ Silent Generation	1925–1945	Loyal, conservative, traditional values. Shaped by Great Depression and World War II. Very few still active in the workforce.
Baby Boomers	1946–1964	Optimistic, career driven, rewards motivated. Shaped by Vietnam War and civil rights movement. Many have begun to retire.
Generation X	1965–1979	Flexible, independent, skeptical. Shaped by introduction of the personal computer, MTV, and the fall of the Soviet Union. In their prime earning years.

Generational Cohort Name	Birth Years	Key Characteristics
Generation Y/ Millennials	1980–1994	Tech savvy, seek purposeful work. Shaped by dot-com crash, 9/11, and the introduction of the iPhone. Largest cohort in workforce and assuming management roles.
Generation Z	1995–2012	Digital natives, value diversity, globally connected. Shaped by social justice, climate change, and global pandemic. Newest cohort to enter workforce.

In conclusion, understanding the different generational cohorts is important for employers seeking to create inclusive and effective workplaces that accommodate the needs and expectations of employees across all generations. It is also critical in leveraging the strengths and attributes of each cohort. This foundational understanding sets the stage for a deeper exploration of Gen Z and the challenges and opportunities they bring to today's workforce, which will be discussed in the next chapter.

Reflective Exercises for Chapter 1: GENERATIONAL PERSPECTIVES

To better understand the generational dynamics in your workplace, take a moment to reflect on your own generational perspective. Consider the following questions:

1. **Generational Perspectives:** Which generational cohort do you belong to (e.g., Baby Boomers, Generation X, Millennials, Generation Z), and how do you think this influences your approach to work and communication?

_____
_____
_____
_____
_____
_____
_____
_____
_____
_____
_____
_____
_____
_____
_____
_____

2. **Generational Differences:** Think about a recent interaction with a colleague from a different generation. How did different generational perspectives influence the interaction? Was the outcome positive or negative?

_____
_____
_____
_____
_____
_____
_____
_____
_____
_____
_____
_____
_____
_____
_____
_____
_____

3. **Bridging Generational Gaps:** What steps can you think of to bridge generational gaps and foster better understanding and collaboration in your workplace?

_____
_____
_____
_____
_____
_____
_____
_____
_____
_____
_____
_____
_____
_____
_____
_____
_____

CHAPTER TWO

Challenges & Opportunities of Gen Z in the Workplace

In my consulting practice, I have seen a variety of challenges that employers face with Gen Z employees. Some common concerns voiced were related to Gen Z's lack of company loyalty, communication issues, heightened focus on mental health concerns, need for frequent feedback and guidance, and strong emphasis on personal time and work–life balance. As Gen Z increasingly enter the workforce, organizations will face many of these and other challenges.

The Challenges of Gen Z in the Workplace

To give you a better understanding of potential issues employers are facing with Gen Z, I have presented a few that often come up. To be fair and balance things out, I have also highlighted some of the advantages I feel that Gen Z offer. As you progress through this book, keep these themes in the back of your mind, as they will be beneficial in helping you develop your own actionable strategies for the workplace.

Communication & Multigenerational Conflict: With up to five different generational cohorts working alongside one another, communication, work styles, teamwork, and collaboration can present unique challenges. As I stated in Chapter 1, each cohort demonstrates unique attitudes, values, and characteristics. If these are not correctly understood and effectively managed, it can lead to tension, conflicts, and misunderstandings. Gen Z, as digital natives, are at ease using digital communication platforms, preferring short messages via text, social media, and mobile apps. This contrasts with older generations that may prefer traditional communication methods, such as face-to-face meetings, emails, and telephone conversations. Misunderstandings could occur over something as simple as the interpretation of a word or even an emoji. These differences can lead to frustrations and impact workflow processes if not properly mitigated.

Need for Instant Feedback: Gen Z has grown up in a world of instant gratification through social media, messaging apps, and on-demand services; just look at platforms like Uber Eats, Netflix, and Spotify. These same expectations are often transported into the workplace. Gen Z expect quick responses and often require frequent validation, causing them to seem impatient. This impacts response time from colleagues and feedback from supervisors. For example, traditional performance review systems and infrequent feedback may fuel uncertainty, anxiety, and job dissatisfaction. This poses a challenge to employers, which may need to adjust the frequency of feedback to ensure employee satisfaction.

Mental Health Concerns: Mental health is a critical concern for Gen Z. A 2024 Deloitte report found that 40% of Gen Z were stressed all or most of the time. Compared to previous generational cohorts, Gen Z demonstrate higher levels of anxiety and depression and are considered one of the most fragile in terms of mental health. In a 2022 McKinsey report, 55% of Gen Z had reported diagnosis or treatment for mental health. Accordingly, Gen Z prioritize their mental and physical well-being, with time away from work important to them. Balancing career success without encroaching on personal time can be challenging, leading to higher absenteeism and turnover rates if left unchecked.

Company Loyalty: Another challenge is Gen Z's relatively low company loyalty. Gen Z are changing jobs at exceptionally high rates compared to other generational cohorts. This leads to increased training and recruitment costs and reduces productivity, disrupts workflow, and breaks team cohesion. The constant need to onboard new employees can also become a strain on HR managers and company resources. With less loyalty, Gen Z are less inclined to go above and beyond in the workplace. Most do not consider their work to be a significant part of their identity compared to prior cohorts. Finding ways to provide an engaging work environment and meeting their needs will enable employers to better recruit and retain their Gen Z talent.

Strengths of Gen Z in the Workplace

Despite some of these challenges, Gen Z also offer many valuable skills to today's work environment that can improve organizational capabilities and culture. This includes their tech savviness, commitment to diversity and inclusion, and global connectivity. As you will discover, this can help drive organizational innovation and foster a more inclusive work environment. Let's look briefly at some of their positive influences.

Diversity and Inclusion: As one of the most diverse generational cohorts yet, Gen Z places high importance on diversity and inclusion. They value a wide range of backgrounds, including ethnicity, gender, and sexual orientation. Gen Z are at the forefront when it comes to social justice and equality and expect their workplaces to be fair and inclusive. Being open to diverse perspectives can be an asset to organizations seeking to create more collaborative and innovative environments. This commitment to diversity can help build an inclusive organizational culture that attracts top talent.

Tech Savviness: As digital natives, Gen Z are at ease with the latest technology, with a seamless ability to multitask and integrate various tools and apps. Gen Z's facility with social media and other forms of digital communication can help organizations remain competitive in an ever-evolving digital world. Their ability to adopt new technologies can drive innovation. Gen Z may be able to provide guidance and assistance to members of older generational cohorts in technology adoption, training, and learning. This is a significant asset to organizations undergoing digital transformation.

Global Perspective: Gen Z has a broader worldview shaped by global connectivity and exposure to diverse cultures. The internet and social media have amplified this. This makes them more culturally competent and aware of world issues, which is an asset in a globalized economy. This global perspective enhances collaboration within multicultural teams and promotes international cooperation. Additionally, Gen Z's commitment to social and environmental causes can guide organizations toward more sustainable and ethical practices. Gen Z's contributions position them as a dynamic and transformative force in the modern workforce.

In summary, by understanding both the challenges and opportunities of Gen Z, organizations can better create environments to support them and leverage their strengths for mutual success. I've presented some of these to provide background context for you to think about before we examine Gen Z's work values and workplace preferences in the next chapter. Remember, take the time you need to go through these learning modules and do the reflective exercises. It is preferable to do them after each chapter, but you can always do them at the end of reading this book. You will gain valuable insights from them. Trust me!

Reflective Exercises Chapter 2: CHALLENGES AND OPPORTUNITIES OF GEN Z IN THE WORKPLACE

Reflect on the following questions to better understand the unique challenges and opportunities Gen Z bring to the workplace.

1. **Challenges of Gen Z in the Workplace**: Have you observed or encountered any specific challenges Gen Z pose in your workplace? If so, how can these be addressed?

_____

_____

_____

_____

_____

_____

_____

_____

_____

_____

_____

_____

_____

_____

_____

_____

_____

2. **Advantages of Gen Z in the Workplace**: What is a unique strength or advantage you have observed Gen Z bring to the workplace, and how has it positively impacted your work environment?

_____
_____
_____
_____
_____
_____
_____
_____
_____
_____
_____
_____
_____
_____
_____
_____
_____
_____

CHAPTER 3

Gen Z Work Value Preferences

Generation Z brings its own unique set of values and expectations to the workplace. Understanding these is critical for employers and managers who want to effectively attract, retain, and engage Gen Z employees. In this chapter, I outline the key findings from my research on the work value preferences of U.S. Gen Z. I wanted to understand what adult Gen Z (18–26 years old) at the time of my study really placed the most importance on in the workplace. This is the most technical chapter in terms of data and results, but again, understanding this will provide you with significant insights to develop your own strategies for success when dealing with Gen Z in the workplace. By understanding Gen Z work values, you will also better understand the basis of and appreciate my recommendations in the following chapter.

Work Values

Work values relate to what someone considers important in the workplace and are inextricably linked to personal values. These values remain relatively constant over the lifetime and play a significant role in workplace motivation, job satisfaction, employee performance, and organizational fit. By understanding Gen Z's work values, we can better adapt workplace strategies to align with them.

The four main work value dimensions, or categories, are as follows:

- **Cognitive** (Intrinsic): The intellectual aspects of the work, often deriving from the nature of the work itself and personal growth.
- **Instrumental** (Extrinsic): The material aspects of the work and tangible rewards, such as compensation, benefits, and job security.
- **Social/Altruistic**: Helping others, positive relations with coworkers, and making positive contributions to society.
- **Prestige**: Aspects of power, status, and authority.

To reiterate, Gen Z work values influence workplace motivation and job satisfaction, which play a central role in workplace recruitment and retention strategies.

Top Work Value Preferences

My research showed that Gen Z placed the highest level of importance on **instrumental** (extrinsic) work values, meaning the tangible or material aspects of the work environment. Some of the top factors that Gen Z considered important included the following:

- Doing work that affords a good **salary**,
- Having access to the **information** needed to do the job,
- Working in an environment that allows for work–life **balance**,
- Having **hours of work** that are convenient,
- The assurance of **job security**,
- Having **benefits** (vacation pay, health/dental insurance pension plan, etc.), and
- Working for a **supportive supervisor** who is considerate.

The top Instrumental factor was a good salary. **Show Gen Z the money!**

Second-Place Work Value Preferences

The second highest category of work value preferences for Gen Z was **cognitive** (intrinsic), relating to the intellectual aspects and nature of the work itself. Some of the top factors Gen Z considered important included the following:

- Having an opportunity for **advancement** in one's career
- Doing work that is **interesting**, exciting, and engaging
- Having the **freedom** to make decisions about how to do work and spend time
- Having an opportunity to **continuously learn** and develop new knowledge

- Doing work that provides a personal sense of **achievement** in one's accomplishments

Third-Place Work Value Preferences

Ranking third in terms of level of importance to Gen Z were **social/altruistic** work values, which related to the social aspect of the work environment and performing work that had a positive impact. This included factors such as

- Doing work that allows for a lot of **social interactions**,
- Working in an environment that is lively and **fun**, and
- Working with agreeable and friendly **coworkers** where one could form friendships.

Gen Z did not find these work values as important as instrumental (#1) and cognitive (#2), emphasizing their ability to separate their personal lives from their work lives. Although Gen Z are often portrayed as being deeply committed to social and environmental causes, I did not find this to be a top work priority for them.

Least Important Work Values

The least important work value dimension was **prestige**, relating to power, control and authority. This included elements such as

- Doing work that is **prestigious** and regarded highly by others,

- Having the **authority** to organize and direct others, and
- Having the ability to **influence** organizational outcomes.

Given these work values ranked lowest, they are not the most effective motivators compared to instrumental and cognitive work values.

Preferences of Gen Z

Work Value Dimension	Ranking
Instrumental	1
Cognitive	2
Social/Altruistic	3
Prestige	4

The work values ranking provides a wealth of insight into the inner forces driving Gen Z and what they care about. These can be used to develop strategies that are best aligned with their preferences to create greater personal fulfilment, job satisfaction, and workplace motivation.

Demographic Variables

Now, you might be wondering, what about gender, ethnicity, or other demographic variables? Do any of those factors impact Gen Z work values? Meaning, do Gen Z members differ by gender in work value preferences? What about ethnic background? I thought the same thing, so I examined several demographic variables in detail: **gender, ethnicity, education level, income level,** and **geographic location** (within the United States).

Gender: There was no difference between male, female, and nonbinary Gen Z in work value preferences. They all rated the four work value dimensions in the same order of preference; top was **instrumental**, followed by **cognitive, social/altruistic,** and **prestige.** Interestingly, both male and female Gen Z placed the highest importance on a good **salary**, as outlined. Nonbinary Gen Z also considered salary important, but their top individual factors were all instrumental: convenient hours of work and access to information and resources to complete one's job.

Ethnicity: We know that Gen Z is one of the most ethnically diverse generations. This might explain why ethnicity was not a factor influencing what Gen Z placed importance on in the workplace. No significant differences in work values were found between the major ethnic groups (Caucasian/White, African American, Native American, Latino/Hispanic, Asian, and Middle Eastern). Even upon grouping the data into Caucasian/White and non-White, no significant differences appeared.

Income, Education, and Geographic Location

Further data analysis did not uncover any differences for other factors, such as annual **income**, **education** level, or **location** (home state). Given that most participants for my study resided in Texas, Florida, California, and New York, I thought it might be interesting to examine the data using traditional "red" versus "blue" states (where voters typically support the Republican Party or Democratic Party, respectively). Again, Gen Z did not seem to not seem to differ based on political affiliation.

> **No demographic variables impacted Gen Z work values!**

In summary, Gen Z demonstrated homogeneity and cohesiveness as a group in terms of work values (principles that guide an individual's behavior and decisions in a professional setting). Factors such as gender, ethnicity, education level, annual income, or state of residence did not have an impact. Knowledge of this information was a key driver in developing effective strategies to better recruit, retain, and motivate Gen Z in the workplace. In the next chapter, I will walk you through my practical recommendations for employers to create a more positive and fulfilling work environment.

Reflective Exercises for Chapter 3: GEN Z WORK VALUES

Reflect on the following question to better understand Gen Z's work values and how they influence workplace dynamics.

1. **Organizational Culture**: How does your organizational culture align with Gen Z's work values and expectations? Could any areas be improved to create a more appealing work environment for them?

___
___
___
___
___
___
___
___
___
___
___
___
___
___
___
___
___
___

2. **Engagement and Motivation**: In what ways does your organization engage and motivate Gen Z employees?

CHAPTER 4

Engaging Gen Z in the Workplace

The work value preferences of Gen Z have major implications for employers, managers, and HR practitioners. To effectively recruit, retain, and engage Gen Z, organizations may wish to analyze and adjust their practices to better align with the work value preferences of this newest generational cohort. I recommended taking a holistic approach and considering the impact any new strategies might have on the other cohorts. The work values preferences outlined in the previous chapter provide evidence-based support for the recommendation I am about to present. I call these the **Four Pillars** for employers if they want to effectively engage Gen Z:

- **Compensation**
- **Work–Life Balance**
- **Stable and Supportive Work Environment**
- **Growth and Interesting Work**

Each pillar encompasses specific elements that organizations can assess and implement to attract and retain Gen Z talent effectively. By focusing on these areas, employers can create a more appealing and motivating work environment for Gen Z. Let's go through the Four Pillars.

First Pillar: Compensation

Salaries: Gen Z place high importance on fair and competitive salaries. Regular reviews and adjustments to salary structures should be performed to ensure they reflect current market rates and the increased cost of living. A Deloitte study found that cost of living is a top concern to Gen Z, with 30% feeling financially insecure, making money a key stressor to them. To highlight the importance Gen Z place on salary, they would select a higher-paying job over one that has a pleasant work atmosphere. Employers should ensure competitive salaries, transparency regarding salary determination, and periodic reviews to attract and retain top Gen Z talent.

Benefits: Comprehensive benefit packages are also of great importance to Gen Z. Health insurance, improved vacation pay, pensions plans, and mental health support are components employers should focus on. Offering a variety of choices through cafeteria-style benefit plans and fringe benefits, such as gym access, paid birthday leave, or subsidized transportation, could resonate well with Gen Z.

Financial Rewards: Gen Z also appreciates financial rewards, such as bonuses, stock option plans, and profit-sharing plans. These incentives align well with their desire for tangible motivators and financial gain. Providing performance-based bonuses and opportunities to buy company stock can help motivate and retain them. Additionally, offering comprehensive retirement plans, such as 401(k) matching (in the United States) or employer-matched RRSP contributions (in Canada), can further support Gen Z's long-term financial security concerns and commitment to the organization.

In Practice

- Regularly review and evaluate salary structures.
- Examine benefit plans in terms of comprehensiveness (health insurance, dental, and improved vacation pay).
- Evaluate company financial reward programs, such as bonuses and stock option plans.

Second Pillar: Work-Life Balance

Flexible Work Schedules: Flexibility in work schedules is another top priority for Gen Z. They place high importance on balancing their personal and professional lives. Flexible schedules can improve Gen Z's job satisfaction and productivity. Establishing work policies that allow for less rigidity and more flexibility (schedules, hours of work, remote work) that meet individual needs will be seen as an asset.

Convenient Work Hours: Convenient working hours that accommodate personal time and well-being are essential to Gen Z. Employers have a variety of approaches to allow employees to adjust their work hours and schedules: staggered hours (choosing different start/end times), compressed workweeks (working longer days for fewer days), core hours (required presence during specific hours in a day), flextime (flexible start/end times within a range), telecommuting (working from home), and part-time work (working fewer hours per week). These arrangements can help Gen Z employees balance their personal commitments while maintaining team collaboration and organizational goals.

Remote/Hybrid Work: Gen Z began their careers in an era of remote and hybrid work, making this not only the norm but highly appealing. Gen Z do want to go into the office from time to time, but having ability to work remotely is also critical. It supports their preference for work–life balance and flexibility in their schedules. Gen Z want to be able to take a break during the day to enjoy a walk or other personal activity. A hybrid work model is therefore highly appealing. Employers should provide the resources, technology, and support for effective remote work environment. This includes information technology (IT) support, establishing clear expectations, and regular check-ins with employees to avoid feelings of isolation.

Wellness Programs: Providing comprehensive wellness programs that focus on both physical and mental health is vital to Gen Z. These programs should include mental health support, stress management resources, and fitness initiatives to promote overall well-being. Organizations can offer a range of solutions, such as counseling services, massage therapy, and designated relaxation spaces. Workshops on mindfulness and stress management can further support mental health. Additionally, healthy snacks and food options in the office and discounts on gym memberships or access to an on-site gym can enhance physical wellness. If Gen Z do not feel that an organization provides enough work–life balance and support in terms of wellness, they may opt to leave for companies that do.

In Practice:

- Allow for flexible work schedules and convenient hours.
- Offer remote and/or hybrid work options.
- Develop comprehensive wellness programs, including physical and mental health.

Third Pillar: Stable & Supportive Work Environment

Job Security: Job security is a top concern for Gen Z. Providing clear communication about their long-term career prospects and job stability will be essential in reducing their concerns. Offering full-time employment, as opposed to contract work, will also greatly help to keep Gen Z motivated at work and reduce their financial anxiety. In the 2024 Deloitte study, six out of 10 Gen Z said they lived paycheck to paycheck, highlighting the financial insecurity they are experiencing. Providing job security and a steady paycheck will allow Gen Z to focus on their work and develop their careers within the organization.

Resources and Support: Providing the necessary resources and tools for job performance is crucial for Gen Z. Access to the latest technology and tools enables them to work effectively. Employers should also offer ongoing training and proper support to ensure high levels of productivity and job satisfaction. IT support is essential to resolve issues promptly and minimize work interruptions. Attention should also be given to the physical environment to ensure comfort and well-being. Organizations may also wish to implement mentorship programs where more experienced workers guide Gen Z as they enter the workplace. This can serve a dual purpose through reverse mentoring, where senior employees learn from Gen Z perspectives, ultimately enhancing the organizational culture.

Supportive Supervision: Gen Z seeks supportive supervisors who offer them feedback, encouragement, and guidance. Managers should act more like coaches, with a personalized one-on-one and collaborative approach. Providing ongoing support to Gen Z and casually engaging in frequent and constructive dialogue will be effective at retaining and motivating Gen Z workers. It would be advisable to develop their strengths and focus on areas of improvement. Supervisors should have open lines of communication and be accessible to Gen Z.

In Practice:

- Ensure job security through transparent communication and stable contracts.
- Provide necessary resources and technology for job performance.
- Foster a culture of support and open communication.
- Create opportunities for personalized coaching and mentorship.

Fourth Pillar: Growth & Interesting Work

Stimulating & Challenging Work: Gen Z seeks work that is stimulating and challenging. They are motivated by tasks that push their boundaries and allow them to use their skills creatively. Gen Z desire the freedom to make decisions about how they work and opportunities to problem-solve and take ownership of work projects. Employers should avoid assigning routine or monotonous work, instead exposing them to various aspects of the company. Employers should also offer opportunities for Gen Z to take on new and exciting projects. This will cater to Gen Z's desire for interesting work within the organization.

Opportunities for Advancement: Gen Z values opportunities for growth and advancement within the organization. Employers should provide guidance and discuss career development. They should also communicate openings and encourage Gen Z employees to apply for higher-level organizational positions. Additionally, employers can offer possibilities for Gen Z to develop their work skills and acquire new knowledge relevant to their career goals. Job rotation across various departments and mentorship programs are other methods of providing a broader understanding of the organization and inspiring them to pursue advancement.

Continuing Education & Learning: Offering opportunities for continuing education and professional development is important to Gen Z, as they are eager to develop their skills. Employers can provide learning opportunities through in-person or self-paced online courses, workshops, and conferences. Encouraging Gen Z to acquire industry credentials and certifications would be beneficial and respond to their needs for learning. Additionally, employers could offer tuition reimbursement.

Positive Onboarding Experience: Creating a positive onboarding experience tailored for Gen Z is important. Clearly and realistically outlining job functions during onboarding can help manage their expectations and reduce turnover. Employers should implement an engaging onboarding program that is personalized, comprehensive, and clear about job expectations and company culture. Ensuring a welcoming and positive environment will provide the best chance for long-term success.

In Practice:

- Design jobs that are stimulating and challenging.
- Provide clear career advancement opportunities.

- Offer continuing education and learning programs.
- Create a positive onboarding experience.

In summary, to create the most engaging and rewarding environment for Gen Z, employers must consider their unique characteristics. Employers should examine their management practices and be responsive to the changing needs and preferences of Gen Z. By offering competitive compensation, work–life balance, a stable and supportive work environment, growth opportunities, and stimulating work, employers can create a workplace that resonates with Gen Z's values and aspirations. These efforts not only enhance job satisfaction and productivity but also contribute to a more engaged and loyal workforce.

Self-Reflective Exercises for Chapter 4: ENGAGING GEN Z IN THE WORKPLACE

Reflect on the following questions to understand how your organization can better align with the work value preferences of Gen Z.

1. **Compensation**
   - **Salaries**: How does your organization ensure salaries are competitive and fair? What steps can be taken to enhance transparency in salary determination and regular reviews?

   _____
   _____
   _____
   _____
   _____
   _____
   _____
   _____
   _____
   _____
   _____
   _____
   _____
   _____
   _____
   _____
   _____
   _____
   _____

- **Benefits**: What types of benefits does your organization offer? How can these be improved to meet the expectations of Gen Z, particularly regarding health insurance and mental health support?

_____
_____
_____
_____
_____
_____
_____
_____
_____
_____
_____
_____
_____
_____
_____
_____

- **Financial Rewards**: How does your organization use financial rewards, such as bonuses and stock options? What incentives could be introduced to better motivate Gen Z?

_____
_____
_____
_____
_____
_____
_____
_____
_____
_____
_____
_____
_____
_____
_____

2. **Work–Life Balance**
   - **Flexible Work Schedules**: How flexible are the work schedules in your organization? What policies could be implemented to allow for more personalized and flexible work hours?

   _____
   _____
   _____
   _____
   _____
   _____
   _____
   _____
   _____
   _____
   _____
   _____
   _____
   _____
   _____
   _____
   _____
   _____
   _____

- **Remote/Hybrid Work**: How effectively does your organization support remote and hybrid work models? What improvements can be made to provide the necessary technology and support for remote work?

- **Wellness Programs**: What wellness programs does your organization offer? How can these programs be enhanced to focus more on both physical and mental health?

_____
_____
_____
_____
_____
_____
_____
_____
_____
_____
_____
_____
_____
_____
_____
_____
_____
_____

3. **Stable & Supportive Work Environment**
   - **Job Security**: How does your organization communicate job stability and long-term career prospects to employees?

   _____
   _____
   _____
   _____
   _____
   _____
   _____
   _____
   _____
   _____
   _____
   _____
   _____
   _____
   _____
   _____
   _____

- **Supportive Supervision**: How do supervisors in your organization support Gen Z employees? What training or resources could help supervisors provide better guidance and feedback?

_____
_____
_____
_____
_____
_____
_____
_____
_____
_____
_____
_____
_____
_____
_____
_____

- **Resources and Support**: How well does your organization provide the necessary resources and technology for job performance? What additional resources or support could improve productivity and satisfaction?

_____
_____
_____
_____
_____
_____
_____
_____
_____
_____
_____
_____
_____
_____
_____
_____
_____
_____

- **Mentorship Programs**: Does your organization have mentorship programs? If so, how could they be enhanced to better support and develop Gen Z employees? If not, how could one be established?

_____
_____
_____
_____
_____
_____
_____
_____
_____
_____
_____
_____
_____
_____
_____
_____
_____

4. **Growth & Interesting Work**
   - **Stimulating & Challenging Work**: How does your organization ensure that jobs are stimulating and challenging for Gen Z employees? What opportunities can be provided to allow them to take on new and exciting projects?

   _____
   _____
   _____
   _____
   _____
   _____
   _____
   _____
   _____
   _____
   _____
   _____
   _____
   _____
   _____
   _____
   _____

- **Opportunities for Advancement**: How clear and attainable are the career advancement paths in your organization? What can be done to provide regular career development discussions and promote from within?

_____

_____

_____

_____

_____

_____

_____

_____

_____

_____

_____

_____

_____

_____

_____

_____

- **Continuing Education & Learning**: What opportunities for continuing education and professional development does your organization offer? How can these be expanded to support Gen Z's eagerness to learn and improve their skills?

_____
_____
_____
_____
_____
_____
_____
_____
_____
_____
_____
_____
_____
_____
_____

- **Onboarding Experience**: How can your organization improve its onboarding process to ensure a positive and engaging experience for new Gen Z employees, to set them up for long-term success?

_____
_____
_____
_____
_____
_____
_____
_____
_____
_____
_____
_____
_____
_____
_____
_____
_____

CHAPTER 5

Embracing the Future of Work with Gen Z

This book has explored the unique characteristics, challenges, and opportunities associated with Gen Z in the workplace. You have learned that they are the most diverse and tech-savvy generational cohort yet. As they become an increasingly dominant force in the workplace, you will be better equipped to develop strategies that align with their values for improved engagement and productivity.

Summary of Key Points
In this final chapter, I will summarize the key ideas that were presented in this book. As you navigate your own multigenerational workplace, you may find it helpful to revisit this chapter from time to time. You can view it as your own

personal executive summary. You may also wish to explore your answers to the self-reflective exercises and retake them. By understanding the concepts in this book, you will be prepared to create a more engaging and collaborative environment that resonates with Gen Z.

Generational Cohorts in the Workplace: Today's workplace consists of several generational cohorts, each one bringing its own set of values, beliefs, and characteristics. This will influence workplace preferences and expectations. To create a productive and collaborative work environment, you will need to consider the unique traits and values of each cohort. The Traditionalists (born 1925–1945) are frugal and loyal, preferring stability and top-down management. Baby Boomers (born 1946–1964) are career driven and respect authority but are retiring in large numbers. Generation X (born 1965–1979) are independent and adaptable, bridging the analog and digital worlds. Millennials (born 1980–1994) value meaningful work, prefer collaborative environments, and are now assuming leadership roles in organizations. Generation Z (born 1995–2012), the newest cohort, are tech-savvy digital natives who prioritize social justice and diversity but face challenges with social skills and mental health. By appreciating the diverse experiences and expectations of each generation, organizations can build more effective and inclusive teams, promoting collaboration and reducing potential conflicts.

Challenges and Opportunities with Gen Z: Employers face unique challenges with Gen Z. These include concerns about their lack of perceived company loyalty, communication issues, mental health, need for frequent feedback, and emphasis on work–life balance. These can lead to generational conflict and misunderstandings and impact management strategies for employee retention and engagement. Gen Z's preference for digital communication can clash with older generations' methods, and their desire for instant feedback can strain traditional performance review systems. Mental health is a significant concern, with high levels of anxiety and depression reported. Additionally, their low company loyalty results in higher turnover rates, increasing recruitment and training costs. However, Gen Z also brings valuable strengths. Not only do they possess a youthful energy, they offer tech savviness, commitment to diversity and inclusion, and a global perspective. These strengths can drive organizational innovation, create a more inclusive work environment, and improve global cooperation. Leveraging Gen Z's positive attributes can help organizations remain competitive in a rapidly changing world.

Gen Z Work Values: Work values are aspects of the work environment that individuals consider important, impacting motivation, job satisfaction, and organizational fit. U.S. adult Gen Z members place highest importance on instrumental (extrinsic) values, which relate to having a good salary, job security, and work–life balance. Cognitive (intrinsic) values, which include factors such as career advancement, and performing interesting work, follow in importance. Social/altruistic work values, which include factors such as social interactions and a lively work environment, ranked third.

Prestige work values, which relate to aspects of power and authority, were least important. Demographic factors, such as gender, ethnicity, education level, income, and geographic location, did not influence these work value preferences, indicating a cohesive set of values across the Gen Z cohort. Understanding these preferences is crucial for developing strategies to create a more engaging and satisfying work environment for Gen Z employees.

Key Recommendations for Employers: It is critical to create workplace strategies that are aligned with the work value preferences of Gen Z to better recruit, retain, and motivate. Employers, managers, and HR practitioners are encouraged to analyze and adjust their workplace practices to better suit Gen Z's unique needs and preferences. I presented a framework to help you develop effective workplace engagement strategies for Gen Z, which is the **Four Pillars—Compensation, Work–Life Balance, Stable & Supportive Work Environment, and Growth & Interesting Work**. To address the first pillar, employers should offer fair and competitive salaries, comprehensive benefits, and financial rewards, such as bonuses and stock options. For the second pillar, employers should examine flexibility in work schedules and the option for remote or hybrid work. They should also establish comprehensive wellness programs focusing on both physical and mental health. Regarding the third pillar, employers should offer job security and access to necessary resources and support. They should also ensure supportive supervision and clear communication about career prospects to reduce Gen Z's anxiety and maintain motivation.

For the fourth pillar, employers should make sure to offer stimulating and challenging work that allows for creative problem-solving and career advancement opportunities. Employers should provide clear pathways for growth, job rotation, mentorship programs, and continuing education opportunities. Creating a positive onboarding experience with a personalized and comprehensive program that clearly outlines job expectations and company culture is also crucial. By focusing on these areas, employers can create a more appealing and motivating work environment for Gen Z, enhancing job satisfaction, productivity, and loyalty. These efforts not only benefit Gen Z employees but also contribute to a more engaged and effective workforce overall.

Future Trends and Considerations

As you look ahead, several emerging trends will continue to influence the workplace, including the increase in hybrid/remote and decentralized work models. The pandemic accelerated this trend, with no slowdown in sight. Flexible workspaces and coworking arrangements will likely be on the rise as organizations look to reduce physical square footage and cut costs. This offers flexibility to employees and allows employers to access a larger talent pool. Companies will also likely adopt more freelancers and contractors, allowing for greater flexibility. Gen Z's work preferences will continue to disrupt and challenge the traditional 9–5 work concept.

Employee well-being will also continue to gain importance, as improved mental and physical health is critical for a productive and happy workforce. Wellness programs will therefore increasingly play a vital role in keeping employees and the newest hires motivated and engaged. This includes programs to promote physical and mental health in the workplace. Preventive care will also become increasingly standard to ensure employee health. Increased access to resources and paid time off will also likely grow. Part of employee well-being is a focus on creating an inclusive environment. Fostering an inclusive and diverse environment that promotes fairness and equality where employees feel respected will continue to be a top priority.

Artificial intelligence (AI) is a significant emerging trend. It will likely transform and revolutionize various aspects of the work environment, from automation of routine tasks to job redesign. Employers will likely need to adjust employee responsibilities and role functions. AI will also impact HR management approaches, including talent acquisition and selection, from screening resumes, to matching candidates to job requirements, to conducting interviews. This will also bring with it a host of ethical concerns regarding bias, transparency, and privacy.

As Gen Z establishes their presence in the workforce, employers should recognize that Gen Alpha (born 2013–2028) is following close behind. This is yet another emerging trend to watch for. The oldest members of Gen Alpha are still teenagers but will soon be entering tomorrow's workplace. They will represent the largest generational cohort in history, entering adulthood in the late 2020s. Gen Alpha are hyperconnected and expected to bring new dynamics, as they are even more tech savvy and accustomed to digital interactions than Gen Z. Employers will need to watch for developing trends and unique characteristics of Gen Alpha and how they might contribute to a multigenerational workforce as Gen Z settles in and begins to assume leadership and management roles.

These trends are just a few aspects of the dynamic world we live in that will transform the workplace and necessitate new approaches to effectively manage and engage a diverse, multigenerational workforce. Staying informed about these and other trends and is of vital importance for employers. Be proactive, and address them head on, which allows you to create a more inclusive, innovative, and resilient work environment that is poised for success.

Call to Action

As a manager, business leader, HR practitioner, or career advisor, you now have the opportunity to use this knowledge to transform the workplace and play a key role in shaping tomorrow's workplace. By understanding the unique work values of Gen Z and implementing the strategies discussed in this book, you can build a more harmonious and productive multigenerational environment. These strategies will not only improve the performance and satisfaction of your Gen Z employees but also benefit other generational cohorts. This will lead to enhanced collaboration and success across the entire organization.

I want to thank you for embarking on this journey. I hope this book has provided you with valuable insights and practical tools to navigate the evolving 21st-century workplace. I want to leave you with one final piece of advice: Embrace the future with an open mind and a commitment to foster an inclusive workplace where every generational cohort can thrive. **Remember, personal differences exist within any generational cohort, so it's important to approach each employee as an individual and not make broad assumptions solely based on generational labels.** However, using my evidence-based insights and Four Pillars framework, you can create a workplace that resonates with Gen Z's values and preferences. By embracing these strategies, you are not only preparing for the future of work but also paving the way for a more dynamic, inclusive, and successful organization.

Final Reflective Exercises for Chapter 5:
KEY TAKEAWAYS

Now that you have concluded this book, take a few moments to reflect on the following questions.

1. **Key Takeaways**: What are the key takeaways you have gained from this book? How do they apply to your role, organization, and work environment?

2. **Implementation of Concepts**: How will you implement the strategies and concepts you learned in this book to improve your multigenerational workplace environment?

_____
_____
_____
_____
_____
_____
_____
_____
_____
_____
_____
_____
_____
_____
_____
_____
_____
_____

3. **Action Plan Priorities**: What changes or actions do you plan to prioritize based on the knowledge you have acquired from this book?

_____

_____

_____

_____

_____

_____

_____

_____

_____

_____

_____

_____

_____

_____

_____

_____

COMPLIMENTARY ONLINE RESOURCES

As I mentioned at the start of this book, as an added bonus and thank-you, I'm offering you complimentary online resources. I encourage you to visit http://www.bierbrier.com/resources to download the entire digital worksheets in PDF format. These resources are designed to help you apply the book's key insights and concepts to your organization and environment, enriching your learning journey. Whether you're exploring new workplace strategies or reinforcing your understanding, these resources are crafted to enhance your experience and empower you to take action in today's multigenerational workplace.

CONNECT WITH THE AUTHOR

I am always happy to hear from my readers and welcome your feedback and insights. If you have any questions or comments or simply want to share your thoughts, please reach out to me through my website: www.bierbrier.com. I greatly value and appreciate reader perspectives.

Additionally, I am available for consulting work, training workshops, and speaking engagements. My consulting practice specializes in organizational development, people, and culture, with a focus on the multigenerational workforce and Gen Z recruitment, motivation, and retention. If you are interested in my services, please feel free to contact me through my website.

ABOUT THE RESEARCH

This book is based on my doctoral dissertation entitled "Work Value Preferences of Generation Z in the United States," which I completed at Johnson & Wales University (Providence, Rhode Island, U.S.). The study aimed to identify the work values most important to Gen Z. Using quantitative research methods, I surveyed 440 U.S. adults, aged 18–26, selected through nonprobabilistic sampling to obtain a representative national sample. Data collection occurred in February 2022. The median age was 22 years, with 52.3% female, 42.5% male, and 4.1% nonbinary; the remainder opted not to specify. The three largest ethnic groups were Caucasian/White (60%), Latino/Hispanic (18%), and African American/Black (11%). Most participants were employed (56%), and the highest percentage earned $25,000–$49,000 (29%).

Data were collected via a self-administered online questionnaire that included both demographic questions and

25 specific work value questions, where participants rated the importance of various factors in accepting or staying in a job. I performed advanced statistical analysis, including confirmatory factor analysis for structural equation modeling, to validate the work values scales and theoretical model, confirming the structure and construct of the work values dimensions.

ABOUT THE AUTHOR

Dr. Charles Bierbrier is a business consultant, professor, and public speaker. He has over 25 years of broad industry experience as an entrepreneur and organizational leader. As a respected lecturer and educator, he has taught business courses at McGill University, Concordia University, and Dawson College in Montreal (Quebec) Canada. He is a well-versed public speaker and has been featured in several magazines and television, and radio shows.

He holds a Doctorate of Business Administration from Johnson & Wales University, a Master of Business Administration from Concordia University, and a Bachelor of Arts in Economics from McGill University.

As an active and involved member of his community, Dr. Bierbrier provides his leadership and expertise on the boards of several nonprofit and community organizations.

FOUR PILLARS FOR GEN Z ENGAGEMENT

Pillar 1	Details
Compensation	**Salaries**: Ensure fair and competitive salaries with regular reviews. Address cost of living concerns as a top stressor for Gen Z.
	Benefits: Offer comprehensive benefit packages, including health insurance, vacation pay, pensions, and mental health support. Consider fringe benefits, such as gym access or paid birthday leave.
	Financial Rewards: Provide financial rewards, such as bonuses, stock options, and profit-sharing plans. Offer performance-based incentives and comprehensive retirement plans.

Pillar 2	Details
Work–Life Balance	**Flexible Work Schedules:** Provide flexibility in work schedules to improve job satisfaction and productivity.
	Convenient Work Hours: Offer staggered hours, compressed workweeks, core hours, flextime, telecommuting, and part-time work options to balance personal commitments.
	Remote/Hybrid Work: Support remote and hybrid work models, providing necessary technology and support.
	Wellness Programs: Develop comprehensive wellness programs focusing on physical and mental health, including stress management and fitness initiatives.

Pillar 3	Details
Stable & Supportive Work Environment	**Job Security:** Ensure clear communication about job stability, and offer full-time employment with steady paychecks.
	Resources and Support: Provide necessary resources and up-to-date technology for job performance.
	Supportive Supervision: Foster a culture of supportive supervision, offering guidance and frequent feedback.
	Coaching and Mentoring: Implement coaching and mentoring programs for professional growth and development.

Pillar 4	Details
Growth & Interesting Work	**Stimulating & Challenging Work:** Offer opportunities for Gen Z to take on new and exciting projects.
	Opportunities for Advancement: Provide clear paths for career advancement, with regular career development discussions.
	Continuing Education & Learning: Offer access to online courses, workshops, and conferences for skill improvement.
	Positive Onboarding Experience: Create a positive and realistic onboarding experience to manage expectations and reduce turnover.

COMPLETE SET OF WORKSHEETS

Reflective Exercises for Chapter 1:
Generational Perspectives

To better understand the generational dynamics in your workplace, take a moment to reflect on your own generational perspective. Consider the following questions:

1. **Generational Perspectives**: Which generational cohort do you belong to (e.g., Baby Boomers, Generation X, Millennials, Generation Z), and how do you think this influences your approach to work and communication?

_____

_____

_____

_____

_____

_____

_____

_____

_____

_____

_____

2. **Generational Differences**: Think about a recent interaction with a colleague from a different generation. How did different generational perspectives influence the interaction? Was the outcome positive or negative?

_____
_____
_____
_____
_____
_____
_____
_____
_____
_____
_____
_____
_____
_____
_____
_____
_____

3. **Bridging Generational Gaps**: What steps can you think of to bridge generational gaps and foster better understanding and collaboration in your workplace?

_____
_____
_____
_____
_____
_____
_____
_____
_____
_____
_____
_____
_____
_____
_____
_____
_____

Reflective Exercises Chapter 2:
Challenges and Opportunities of Gen Z in the Workplace
Reflect on the following questions to better understand the unique challenges and opportunities Gen Z bring to the workplace.

1. **Challenges of Gen Z in the Workplace**: Have you observed or encountered any specific challenges Gen Z pose in your workplace? If so, how can it be addressed?

_____
_____
_____
_____
_____
_____
_____
_____
_____
_____
_____
_____

2. **Advantages of Gen Z in the Workplace**: What is a unique strength or advantage you have observed Gen Z bring to the workplace, and how has it positively impacted your work environment?

_____
_____
_____
_____
_____
_____
_____
_____
_____
_____
_____
_____
_____
_____
_____
_____
_____
_____

Reflective Exercises for Chapter 3:
Gen Z Work Values

Reflect on the following question to better understand Gen Z's work values and how they influence workplace dynamics.

1. **Organizational Culture**: How does your organizational culture align with Gen Z's work values and expectations? Could any areas be improved to create a more appealing work environment for them?

_____

_____

_____

_____

_____

_____

_____

_____

_____

_____

_____

_____

_____

2. **Engagement and Motivation**: In what ways does your organization engage and motivate Gen Z employees?

Self-Reflective Exercises for Chapter 4: Engaging Gen Z in the Workplace

Reflect on the following questions to understand how your organization can better align with the work value preferences of Gen Z.

1. **Compensation**
    - **Salaries:** How does your organization ensure salaries are competitive and fair? What steps can be taken to enhance transparency in salary determination and regular reviews?

    _____
    _____
    _____
    _____
    _____
    _____
    _____
    _____
    _____
    _____
    _____
    _____

- **Benefits**: What types of benefits does your organization offer? How can these be improved to meet the expectations of Gen Z, particularly regarding health insurance and mental health support?

- **Financial Rewards**: How does your organization use financial rewards, such as bonuses and stock options? What incentives could be introduced to better motivate Gen Z?

_____

_____

_____

_____

_____

_____

_____

_____

_____

_____

_____

_____

_____

_____

_____

_____

_____

2. **Work–Life Balance**
   - **Flexible Work Schedules**: How flexible are the work schedules in your organization? What policies could be implemented to allow for more personalized and flexible work hours?

   _____

   _____

   _____

   _____

   _____

   _____

   _____

   _____

   _____

   _____

   _____

   _____

   _____

   _____

   _____

- **Remote/Hybrid Work**: How effectively does your organization support remote and hybrid work models? What improvements can be made to provide the necessary technology and support for remote work?

_____
_____
_____
_____
_____
_____
_____
_____
_____
_____
_____
_____
_____
_____
_____
_____
_____
_____
_____
_____

- **Wellness Programs**: What wellness programs does your organization offer? How can these programs be enhanced to focus more on both physical and mental health?

_____

_____

_____

_____

_____

_____

_____

_____

_____

_____

_____

_____

_____

_____

_____

_____

_____

_____

3. **Stable & Supportive Work Environment**
   - **Job Security**: How does your organization communicate job stability and long-term career prospects to employees?

   _____
   _____
   _____
   _____
   _____
   _____
   _____
   _____
   _____
   _____
   _____
   _____
   _____
   _____
   _____
   _____
   _____

- **Supportive Supervision**: How do supervisors in your organization support Gen Z employees? What training or resources could help supervisors provide better guidance and feedback?

- **Resources and Support**: How well does your organization provide the necessary resources and technology for job performance? What additional resources or support could improve productivity and satisfaction?

_____
_____
_____
_____
_____
_____
_____
_____
_____
_____
_____
_____
_____
_____
_____

- **Mentorship Programs**: Does your organization have mentorship programs? If so, how could they be enhanced to better support and develop Gen Z employees? If not, how could one be established?

4. **Growth & Interesting Work**
   - **Stimulating & Challenging Work**: How does your organization ensure that jobs are stimulating and challenging for Gen Z employees? What opportunities can be provided to allow them to take on new and exciting projects?

   _____
   _____
   _____
   _____
   _____
   _____
   _____
   _____
   _____
   _____
   _____
   _____
   _____
   _____
   _____
   _____

- **Opportunities for Advancement**: How clear and attainable are the career advancement paths in your organization? What can be done to provide regular career development discussions and promote from within?

- **Continuing Education & Learning**: What opportunities for continuing education and professional development does your organization offer? How can these be expanded to support Gen Z's eagerness to learn and improve their skills?

_____

_____

_____

_____

_____

_____

_____

_____

_____

_____

_____

_____

_____

_____

_____

_____

- **Onboarding Experience**: How can your organization improve its onboarding process to ensure a positive and engaging experience for new Gen Z employees, to set them up for long-term success?

Final Reflective Exercises for Chapter 5:
Key Takeaways

Now that you have concluded this book, take a few moments to reflect on the following questions.

1. **Key Takeaways**: What are the key takeaways you have gained from this book? How do they apply to your role, organization, and work environment?

   _____
   _____
   _____
   _____
   _____
   _____
   _____
   _____
   _____
   _____
   _____
   _____
   _____

2. **Implementation of Concepts**: How will you implement the strategies and concepts learned in this book to improve your workplace environment?

3. **Action Plan Priorities**: What changes or actions do you plan to prioritize based on the knowledge you have acquired from this book?

_____
_____
_____
_____
_____
_____
_____
_____
_____
_____
_____
_____
_____
_____
_____
_____
_____

BIBLIOGRAPHY

2023 Gen Z Screen Time Report. (2023). Dcdx. https://dcdx.co/the-2023-gen-z-screen-time-report

Appelbaum, S. H., Bhardwaj, A., Goodyear, M., Gong, T., Sudha, A. B., & Wei, P. (2022). A study of generational conflicts in the workplace. *European Journal of Business and Management Research, 7*(2), 7–15.

Arora, S., Dubey, V., & Vyas, S. (2020). Study of work values of Gen Z students. *International Journal of Technology and Globalisation, 8*(3/4), 240–265. https://doi.org/10.1504/IJTG.2020.10034407

Bierbrier, C. V. (2022). *Work value preferences of Generation Z in the United States.* [Doctoral dissertation, Johnson & Wales University]. https://www.proquest.com/docview/2731703651/A6EA00D6B9724D90PQ/1

Calk, R., & Patrick, A. (2017). Millennials through the looking glass: Workplace motivating factors. *The Journal of Business Inquiry, 16*(2), 131–139.

Campbell, S. M., Twenge, J. M., & Campbell, W. K. (2017). Fuzzy but useful constructs: Making sense of the differences between generations. *Work, Aging and Retirement*, 3(2), 130–139. https://doi.org/10.1093/workar/wax001

Challenges of managing Generation Z in the workplace. (2024, January 30). https://reba.global/resource/4-challenges-of-managing-generation-z-in-the-workplace.html

Civilian labor force, by age, sex, race, and ethnicity. (2023, September 6). Bureau of Labor Statistics. https://www.bls.gov/emp/tables/civilian-labor-force-summary.htm

Deloitte Global 2024 Gen Z and Millennial Survey. (2024). https://www.deloitte.com/global/en/issues/work/content/genz-millennialsurvey.html

Francis, T., & Hoefel, F. (2018, November 12). *"True Gen": Generation Z and its implications for companies*. McKinsey& Company. https://www.mckinsey.com/industries/consumer-packaged-goods/our-insights/true-gen-generation-z-and-its-implications-for-companies

Fry, R. (2018, April 11). Millennials are largest generation in the U.S. labor force. *Pew Research Center*. https://www.pewresearch.org/fact-tank/2018/04/11/millennials-largest-generation-us-labor-force/

Gabrielova, K., & Buchko, A. A. (2021). Here comes Generation Z: Millennials as managers. *Business Horizons*, 64(4), 489–499. https://doi.org/10.1016/j.bushor.2021.02.013

Galloway, S. (2024, April 23). *Gen Zers and millennials are switching jobs at an accelerating pace, and it's paying off. Here's where it can still go wrong*. Fortune. https://fortune.com/2024/04/23/gen-zers-millennials-job-switching-accelerating-pros-cons-careers-employment/

Gomez, K., Mawhinney, T., Betts, K., Sapp, K., Brown, A., & Santner, K. (2019). *Welcome to Generation Z*. Network of Executive Women and Deloitte. https://www2.deloitte.com/content/dam/Deloitte/us/Documents/consumer-business/welcome-to-gen-z.pdf

Graczyk-Kucharska, M., & Erickson, G. S. (2020). A person-organization fit model of Generation Z: Preliminary studies. *Journal of Entrepreneurship, Management and Innovation, 16*(4), 149–176. https://doi.org/10.7341/20201645

Güngör, A., & Alp, G. T. (2019). Generational motivation differences at the R&D centers: Gen Y and Gen Z. *Innovations, 7*(2), 50–53.

Gursoy, D., Maier, T. A., & Chi, C. G. (2008). Generational differences: An examination of work values and generational gaps in the hospitality workforce. *International Journal of Hospitality Management, 27*(3), 448–458. https://doi.org/10.1016/j.ijhm.2007.11.002

Hennelly, D. S., & Schurman, B. (2023, January 5). Bridging generational divides in your workplace. *Harvard Business Review*. https://hbr.org/2023/01/bridging-generational-divides-in-your-workplace

Hey bosses: Here's what Gen Z actually wants at work. (2023, March 26). https://www.deloittedigital.com/us/en/blog-list/2023/gen-z-research-report.html

How does Gen Z see its place in the working world? With trepidation | McKinsey. (2022, October 19). https://www.mckinsey.com/featured-insights/sustainable-inclusive-growth/future-of-america/how-does-gen-z-see-its-place-in-the-working-world-with-trepidation

Howe, N., & Strauss, W. (2000). *Millennials rising: The next great generation.* Vintage.

Lyons, S. T., Higgins, C. A., & Duxbury, L. (2010). Work values: Development of a new three-dimensional structure based on confirmatory smallest space analysis. *Journal of Organizational Behavior, 31*(7), 969–1002. https://doi.org/10.1002/job.658

Maioli, E. (2017). New generations and employment: An exploratory study about tensions between the psycho-social characteristics of the Generation Z and expectations and actions of organizational structures related with employment. *Journal of Business, 2*(1), 1–12.

Marr, B. (2023, October 17). *The 8 biggest future of work trends in 2024 everyone needs to be ready for now.* Forbes. https://www.forbes.com/sites/bernardmarr/2023/10/17/the-8-biggest-future-of-work-trends-in-2024-everyone-needs-to-be-ready-for-now/

McCrindle, M., & Wolfinger, E. (2014). *The ABC of XYZ: Understanding the global generations* (3rd ed.). McCrindle Research.

McRae, E. R., Aykens, P., Lowmaster, K., & Shepp, J. (2024, January 23). 9 Trends that will shape work in 2024 and beyond. *Harvard Business Review.* https://hbr.org/2024/01/9-trends-that-will-shape-work-in-2024-and-beyond

Nix, N. (2021, March 10). Gen Z Workers to triple by 2030, Snap-commissioned report says. *Bloomberg.Com.* https://www.bloomberg.com/news/articles/2021-03-10/gen-z-workers-to-triple-by-2030-snap-commissioned-report-says

Parker, K., & Igielnik, R. (2020, May 14). What we know about Gen Z so far. *Pew Research Center's Social & Demographic Trends Project.* https://www.pewresearch.org/social-trends/2020/05/14/on-the-cusp-of-adulthood-and-facing-an-uncertain-future-what-we-know-about-gen-z-so-far-2/

Pichler, S., Kohli, C., & Granitz, N. (2021). DITTO for Gen Z: A framework for leveraging the uniqueness of the new generation. *Business Horizons, 64*(5), 599–610. https://doi.org/10.1016/j.bushor.2021.02.021

Schroth, H. (2019). Are you ready for Gen Z in the workplace? *California Management Review, 61*(3), 5–18. https://doi.org/10.1177/0008125619841006

Sidorcuka, I., & Chesnovicka, A. (2017). Methods of attraction and retention of generation Z staff. *CBU International Conference Proceedings, 5*, 807–814.

Stillman, D., & Stillman, J. (2017). *Gen Z @ work: How the next generation is transforming the workplace.* Harper Collins.

Strauss, W., & Howe, N. (1991). *Generations: The history of America's future, 1584 to 2069.* William Morrow.

Twenge, J. M. (2017). *iGen: Why today's super-connected kids are growing up less rebellious, more tolerant, less happy—And completely unprepared for adulthood—And what that means for the rest of us.* Simon and Schuster.

Twenge, J. M., & Campbell, S. M. (2008). Generational differences in psychological traits and their impact on the workplace. *Journal of Managerial Psychology, 23*(8), 862–877. https://doi.org/10.1108/02683940810904367

Twenge, J. M., Campbell, S. M., Hoffman, B. J., & Lance, C. E. (2010). Generational differences in work values: Leisure and extrinsic values increasing, social and intrinsic values decreasing. *Journal of Management, 36*(5), 1117–1142. https://doi.org/10.1177/0149206309352246

Understanding Generation Alpha. (2022, July 6). McCrindle. https://mccrindle.com.au/article/topic/generation-alpha/generation-alpha-defined/

Wiedmer, T. (2015). Generations do differ: Best practices in leading Traditionalists, Boomers, and Generations X, Y, and Z. *Delta Kappa Gamma Bulletin, 82*(1), 51–58.

Wilkie, D. (2024, February 9). *Managing the next generation.* SHRM. https://www.shrm.org/topics-tools/news/managing-smart/managing-the-next-generation

www.ingramcontent.com/pod-product-compliance
Lightning Source LLC
Chambersburg PA
CBHW070031040426
42333CB00040B/1462